From the Hillside

Story by Kathryn Sutherland

Illustrated by Lisa Simmons

AF605538

Contents

Chapter 1 – Anna

Mum watched Anna wander to the back corner of the yard, sketchbook in hand, and was saddened by how much older her daughter had seemed lately. Not that Anna looked older than her eleven years, but the war had aged her. She seemed more inward now, and spent most of her time alone and quiet. Mum shook her head. Anna had seen things kids shouldn't have to see, and learned things kids shouldn't need to know.

But when Anna reached the tree, Mum saw the old Anna for a moment — the active, long-limbed kid who was up that enormous tree in a matter of seconds, as agile as a monkey. Anna knew that tree so well — she'd learned to climb it almost as soon as she could walk. Mum watched her duck and weave to avoid catching her thin blonde hair on overhanging branches.

Ouch! She'd grown — and so had a pesky little branch above her, now caught in her hair. Anna didn't look towards Mum, but knew she'd be at the window, cursing her hair.

Mum was always at her about her hair — brush it, tie it back, cut it. Anna had given up on her hair long ago. It was thin hair and nothing could make it any other way. To try was a waste of time, and Anna had more important things to do. Anyway, she freed herself from the clutches of this branch without much trouble. But she kept the twig she extracted from her hair, and continued her familiar climb to her thinking branch.

Chapter 2

The Thinking Tree

From her thinking branch, Anna could see right over the valley, across the city below.

She could see across the valley from her bedroom upstairs, too, as they had no immediate neighbours on the remote hillside. But Anna didn't stay inside much. It was always noisy in the house. Dad's rock'n'roll blasting on the stereo competed with Grandpa's radio on maximum volume. Anna understood that people had different ways of trying to deal with the war. The men in her house chose the 'drown-it-out' method. Meanwhile, the rest of the family was probably going deaf.

No, inside was not a thinking kind of place, and Anna was a thinker. The sprawling tree way down the back had always been her special place — her thinking tree. As a small child, she'd sat on the thinking branch and planned adventures over the mountains to exotic lands. At other times, she had imagined herself talking face-to-face with giants standing far below in the valley, and enlisting their help in times of trouble. Her valley could do with their help now.

These days, when Anna sat on her thinking branch, she mostly thought about the city below. She thought about how it was changing and she tried to remember how the buildings had looked before the war. She often wondered what else might change, so she sketched her favourite places and jotted down memories in the fancy hardcover sketchbook given to her by Uncle Malek and Aunty Jana. Her thinking tree wasn't such a happy place these days, but it was a peaceful place and, to Anna, it seemed a safe place.

Today, Anna thought about her aunt and uncle's house. She leaned out of the tree to try and see it, but she couldn't. So she sat back and remembered holiday celebrations in that house — happy days, with no thoughts of war.

Daydreaming, Anna twiddled with the twig she'd pulled from her hair. Her eyes soon focused on it. She noticed the leaves: 'Anna's eyes'. That's what Uncle Malek called them. "What can you see from up there, Anna, with your thousand eyes?" he'd call to her.

It's true, her eyes were the same colour as the leaves on her tree, and a similar shape. Some leaves should go in her sketchbook. Carefully, she placed the twig of leaves between two, crisp white pages then shut the heavy book tight. Ooh! 'Anna's eyes' squashed inside her book! Anna chuckled. She would share the joke with Uncle Malek later.

Her chuckles stopped in an instant. Anna sat upright, alert and listening. She heard gunfire in the valley below — and it didn't seem as far below as usual. Suddenly the thinking tree seemed too close to the valley.

Mum raced outside, demanding Anna get down immediately. At least in the house the radio and Dad's music would drown out the noise of gunfire.

Anna grabbed her sketchbook, descended as deftly as she'd climbed up and charged across the yard. She was inside with the door locked before the men in the house had even heard what was happening.

Chapter 3

Smells

Sitting on her bed, Anna watched a cloud of grey smoke rising out of the valley. Another building gone up in smoke. Another memory. And a smell she could never grow used to. The smell of war.

Shutting the window, Anna tried to remember how the hillside used to smell. She opened her sketchbook and took a sniff of the 'Anna's eyes' she had placed inside. The leaves had a distinctive smell. A pre-war smell. A happy smell.

Chapter 4

Commotion

There was some kind of commotion going on downstairs — then the screech of tyres. Mum was weeping, so Anna went down.

"Where's Dad gone?"

"To get Uncle Malek. Their house was hit."

"Are they all okay?" Anna's heart thumped.

"Aunty Jana's in hospital, but she'll recover. The others are fine. They were lucky to survive. Their neighbours didn't."

"Oh." Anna's eyes scrunched up. "Will Dad be safe?"

"Oh, Anna, I hope so!" Mum's hug was very tight.

It was a long, nervous wait for Dad to return with Uncle Malek and the baby. Anna and her mum raced out to greet them.

"Thank goodness you're safe!" sighed Mum.

"I'll carry your bags," Anna offered.

The adults stared at her blankly. There was an awkward silence.

"There are no bags, honey." Dad said, finally, leaving Anna to work it out for herself.

Both Dad and Uncle Malek had a faraway look in their eyes — a look of fear and disbelief. Anna didn't want to know what they'd seen in the city that day. She held baby Lena close.

Nobody spoke for a long time at dinner. It definitely wasn't a good time to tell Uncle Malek about the squashed 'Anna's eyes'.

Mum tried to lift the mood. "Well, Anna, you'll be happy to know you're going to get an extra long holiday this term. The school has been closed until further notice."

"Oh, great," answered Anna, surprised at how unenthusiastic her voice sounded.

The next few weeks were relatively quiet, even in the house. Dad just didn't feel like playing rock'n'roll music any more. Mum made Grandpa use headphones for his radio so baby Lena could sleep. At the end of the month, Aunty Jana came out of hospital and everyone relaxed a little.

Chapter 5

Remembering and Forgetting

Anna's sketchbook was almost full, bursting with memories. Anna spent hours in the thinking tree every day: drawing, writing and thinking.

Today she tried to sketch the City Hall where she had gone to ballet classes every Saturday for five years. Anna remembered the ornate windows and heavy carved doors. They were a challenge to draw. She enjoyed that. The roof stumped her, though. There had been something fancy on the top — a turret or short spire — she couldn't remember it exactly.

But she clearly remembered her Saturday trips into the city. They were always a treat. After ballet class, Anna and Mum would walk around the shops and sometimes have lunch in a cafe. Or they would walk to the big city park and have a picnic. Anna loved to feed the ducks their leftover bread. Dad was always interested to hear her tales of the day when they got home in the evening, or next day if they'd stayed over at Uncle Malek's. Hmm. That wouldn't happen any more.

It was many months since they had made the journey down to the city. Dance classes stopped last year. Anna wondered whether the ducks in the city park would still be there. She leaned right out of the tree, but couldn't quite see the park. Maybe if she leaned over a little further … She slipped.

It was a long way down.

Mum came rushing out. "Anna, don't move. Are you hurt? Is anything broken?"

"Ouch. My arm hurts where I landed on it. But I'm okay. Oh, no! My pictures!"

Anna, in pain, staggered around the yard chasing pages from her sketchbook. Her mother retrieved some from the steep slope below.

"Did we get all of them?" gasped Mum, flopping down on the grass.

"Most. The City Hall sketch has gone, but I hadn't finished that one. What was on the top? Was it a turret or a spire?"

"A dome with a turret. There was another at the back of the building, but you couldn't see it from the street. It was a lovely building. I hope they can restore it when all this is over."

Mum's eyes welled with tears, as so often happened these days. She sniffed them back before any dripped onto Anna's sketches. "These are wonderful drawings, Anna. Wonderful memories. Keep them safe."

Then she brushed Anna's hair back with her fingers. "You know, if you kept your hair tidy, you could see where you were going. Then maybe you wouldn't fall out of that tree of yours!"

With her arm in a sling, the thinking tree was temporarily off limits. Anna sat in her bedroom overlooking the city. She tried sketching left-handed. It was frustrating: scribble, start again, scribble, give up.

Instead, she turned the pages of the book slowly from start to finish, looking thoughtfully at her memories. A few pages made her smile. One brought a giggle: the twig of 'Anna's eyes', pressed between two crisp, white pages. But most pages were greeted with a stony silence and the slow shake of her head.

Chapter 6

The War Closes In

Mum burst into Anna's bedroom — panicky, tripping over her words. "We've got to get out. Quick! Pack a few things in here. Oh, no, that's too big. This one."

"What?"

"Hurry! We're going!"

"Where?"

"Away!"

Anna's jaw dropped as she realised what her mother meant. She couldn't speak, couldn't move. What — get out? Flee? Leave? For *ever*?

Anna had never let herself prepare for this moment, but now the moment was here. She froze, wide-eyed and open-mouthed.

"Anna! GET MOVING!"

Frozen.

"PLEASE!"

Her mother's words were like a stranger tapping on the window.

Anna didn't want to look, to hear, or to know. "Go away! Leave me alone."

Mum dashed across the room and threw open the bedroom window. "Anna, listen!"

Anna focused on the rumbles and cracks of gunfire, sounds she'd grown so used to that they had become just extra noises in the background — like Grandpa's radio and Dad's music. But today the outside noises were louder than those inside. Her jaw dropped further. "How close?"

"I don't know... too close. We've got to go. Pack only what you need, not too much."

Anna understood the risk to their lives if they stayed, but how could they just walk away from the place where all her life had been? All that she knew, all that was important to her? Her hillside. Her house. Her tree.

"I don't want to go," said Anna, her voice distant and quiet.

"Me either, love, but we have to. It's far too dangerous to stay." Mum was sniffling as she flitted between the doorway, the wardrobe and the bed, her eyes avoiding the window.

"Oh, can't you feel it?" She shuddered.

“A bit,” Anna shrugged, running her fingers slowly, dream-like, across everything on her dressing table. “What about all our stuff? We can’t just leave it.”

“We’ll be back someday ... I hope.” Mum stopped flitting around and gave Anna a big hug. “Come on, love. I’ll help you pack.” She stood at the wardrobe and started throwing clothes onto the bed. “Two pairs of pants: jeans and ...blue or black track pants?”

Anna shrugged. “Black. Where will we go?”

"We'll take a bus to the border; we can't all fit in the car. The bus leaves in ... oh, no, twenty minutes! We have to leave in ten!" Mum was panicking again, flitting around, behaving like an insect stuck at a window pane, not sure which way to go. Anna always helped the bugs escape.

"It's OK, Mum, I'll do it. You'd better pack your own stuff."

"Oh, that's done. I packed weeks ago."

"What?" Anna was furious.

"I'm sorry." She tried to hug Anna, but was pushed away.

"You've been waiting to go!" Tears welled up in Anna's eyes.

"Oh, darling, did you really think we could stay here through all this?" Mum braved a glance at the window — a fireball rose from only a few kilometres away. "OH! We should have left before. I'll go and see if the others are ready, then I'll be back. Hurry up."

Anna took a deep breath and sighed. She could smell the fire. The valley was glowing. She shut the window quickly, then set about packing. Oh, the clothes took up too much space. Where would her treasures go? She decided to wear most of the clothes.

The sling made getting dressed difficult, but when Mum returned, Anna was heavily padded. She tried to squeeze her art set into her bag. Her sketchbook was still on the bed.

"Anna! I said pack only what you need. Life essentials, not things!" Mum threw Anna's art set onto the bed, then her inline skates and CDs.

"They're essential to my life," Anna grumbled, but she knew Mum was right.

Mum picked up the sketchbook. "Take this. Now hurry!"

Seconds later they were running up the street to the bus stop: Mum helping Grandpa, Uncle Malek with Lena, Dad pushing a wheelbarrow full of bags, and Aunty Jana with her arm around Anna.

Chapter 7

One Last Look

Anna turned back to take a final look. “Goodbye, valley. Goodbye, hillside. Goodbye, house. Goodbye, thinking tree. I’ll miss you.”

Suddenly, a thunderous noise took Anna’s breath away. A massive fireball hit precisely where she was looking, leaving a gaping hole in the roof above Anna’s bedroom. Like a hot-air balloon, the fireball ascended from the house: a glorious orange, warm and impressive. And then it disappeared into thin air, leaving a home devastated and lives in limbo.

A strangled whimper was all Anna could manage. She could barely stay on her feet.

Time stood still for Anna, trying to comprehend the situation. Memories flashed past, backed by the image of her favourite tree, now burning. Her thinking branch crashed to the ground, glowing bright with its thousand eyes.

When her heavy sketchbook slipped from under her arm, Anna noticed Aunty Jana pulling her away. "Come on, Anna. We have to catch up to the others."

Grappling for the sketchbook, Anna dislodged the twig of 'Anna's eyes' taken from the thinking tree. She gripped it tightly as she ran, calling out over the hillside, "I'll be back!"